Unicorn Spells

real spells for love, life & laughter

Unicorn Spells

real spells for love, life & laughter

ISBN: 978-1-912511-61-7

Created by Christina Rose

Contributors: Nataly Popovych

Unicorn Spells For....

Unicorn Spell for Sparking Excitement

What you'll need:

* All the colours of the rainbow (or the icing off a chocolate cupcake should do the job!)
* 2 drops of magic waterfall (or warm water will be ok too)
* A candle
* A mixing bowl
* A wooden oak mixing spoon

What to do:

Do you have all your equipment? Then let's begin.
Start by lighting your candle to bring a sense of calm and serenity to your space, you want to cast out any negativity and darkness. Using your spoon and mixing bowl, combine all the colours of the rainbow (or cupcake icing) with the drops of waterfall (or warm water), turn the mixture 10 times going first anticlockwise, and another 5 going clockwise. Allow the heat from the candle to evaporate any negative feelings and move on to the next step of your spell. Use you pinkie finger to scoop a little of the icing and sit it on to your tongue until it dissolves. As the sweetness dissolves in your mouth make a mental list of 5 incredible things in your mind which you would be excited to do... maybe something like travel to India or learn to skydive - let your mind run wild. Open your eyes and follow your dreams.

Fun Fact:

Did you know that is it impossible to catch a unicorn? It is said that a wild unicorn can outrun even the fastest hunter, with some sightings reporting that a unicorn can move up to 100,000,000 UP (Unicorn Power!)

4

Unicorn Spell for Being Easy Going

What you'll need:

1 tablespoon of Unicorn crystals (or bath salts will do)
The ancient music of the Unicorn Mountains
(or a relaxing playlist)
1 bathtub

What to do:

The Unicorn states that there is a stark difference between true relaxation and becoming easy going of the mind, body and soul. To achieve the latter you must possess a bathtub as you'll need to submerge yourself into the magical waters of the Unicorn. To begin, allow the ancient music from the Unicorn Mountains (or relaxing playlist) to drift out and envelop the room. Turn on your hot water and allow the bath to begin to fill and as it does let your thoughts be present. Once the water is the right temperature, sprinkle in 1 tablespoon of Unicorn crystals (or bath salts) and allow them to dissolve before submerging into the waters. As the aromas and warmth surround you, close your eyes and allow those thoughts of stress, worry and being held back by daily chores leave you. The power of the spell will evaporate these feelings leaving behind a laid back, easy going body & soul.

Fun Fact:

Did you know that the Unicorn can experience every single emotion all at once? It is believed that although a Unicorn has this ability, it chooses to ignore any negative or unhelpful emotions to make room for all the pleasures of life.

Unicorn Spell for Being Confident

What you'll need:

* ★ 10 daisies
* ★ A few lines from your favourite poem
* ★ An accomplished solo violinist (or a classical music CD)
* ★ 1 incense burner

What to do:

Every follower of the Unicorn knows that confidence comes from within, and this spell will help generate that self-confidence which can so easily be lost in modern life. Start by lighting your incense, hold it gently and circle your space 5 times, allowing the rich aroma to fill the air. When you are ready to begin place your incense in a holder, take a seat and listen to the sweet music of the violinist (or classical music CD). With the senses heightened you are better able to absorb the spell. As you start to create a daisy chain with your flowers let your mind run away with scenarios of confidence and power, let those feelings rain over you as you create your circle. Once the daisy chain is finished, place it upon your head and complete the spell by reciting the lines from your favourite poem. Very soon you'll be filled with the confidence that is borne from the power of music & magic.

Fun Fact:

A Unicorn's tail is said to be constantly growing; as old hairs fall out and bless the earth with their magical properties, a new hair instantly grows in its place.

Unicorn Spell for Being Patient

What you'll need:

* 1 tablespoon of loose-leaf tea
* 1 teaspoon of golden nectar (or honey)
* 1 handheld mirror
* 1 kettle
* Water
* 1 teacup

What to do:

They say patience is a virtue, and the Unicorn is the most virtuous creature on Earth. This spell may seem simple but it harnesses incredible strength! Begin by filling your kettle with water, all the while considering the reasons why you are doing this spell; what things cause you to lose your patience and how do you intend to change this? Whilst your water is boiling, take a moment to think of an occasion where you have lost your temper - how did it make you feel? Hold that thought in your mind as you decant 1 tablespoon of loose-leaf tea into your teacup. Slowly top it off with boiling water, and as the leaves soak up and expand, let those negative memories vanish forever. Gently stir 1 teaspoon of golden nectar (honey) into your tea and taking your hand held mirror, hold it in front of your face for 10 seconds. During this time allow yourself to completely let go of your worries or anger and really recognise the strength within you. Finish the spell off by taking a sip of your spellbound tea.

Fun Fact:

Did you know that the Unicorn is the most patient and understanding creature to ever exist? It is said that a Unicorn has never lost it's temper in any situation.

Unicorn Spell for Falling In Love

What you'll need:

* 1 mixing bowl
* 1 mixing spoon
* The petals from 1 red rose
* A star from the night sky (or a paper star should do)
* An ancient saxophone (or a jazz CD)
* A small treasure chest (or a matchbox will do!)
* 1 tablespoon of the finest silver (silver glitter should suffice)

What to do:

For this spell you need to concentrate on the object of your love throughout, so ensure you remain focused. Start by playing a few notes on the ancient saxophone (or press play on your CD player). Take your mixing bowl and add in the tablespoon of the finest silver (or silver glitter). Taking the spoon, gently stir the glitter as you think about your true love, sprinkle in all the petals of the red rose, and now stir anticlockwise with your spoon. Finally pluck 1 star from the night sky (or use a paper star) and place this into your bowl. Imagine yourself with your love. As you think how your life will unfold with the two of you together, remove the star and gently pour as much of the mixture as you can into your small treasure chest (matchbox) so that you can carry your spell with you at all times to attract your love to you.

Fun Fact:

Did you know that when a Unicorn finds a partner, it mates for life? Unicorns are each destined to find love that is made only for them. When they find their true love, they remain together forever.

Unicorn Spell for Creativity

What you'll need:

* 3 coloured pencils (the choice is yours)
* A sacred scroll (or a piece of paper will do)
* An image of a Unicorn
* A pair of magical shears (or scissors)

What to do:

Place yourself comfortably on the floor, ensure you have a perfect view of your Unicorn image; this will be your guide throughout the spell. To conjure up the highest levels of creativity you'll want to ensure the space around you is clear of any distractions; it should just be you and your equipment. Take the first coloured pencil from your collection, and closing your eyes begin to draw whatever image is conjured in your mind's eye upon the sacred scroll (paper). When you feel ready, open your eyes to see your creation so far. Now pull energy and inspiration from the Unicorn image in front of you. Close you eyes again and use the second & third coloured pencils to finish your creation. Once you feel it is complete, open your eyes and take a look, using your sheers (scissors) cut out your creation, and place it next to the Unicorn image. You now have a source of creativity to turn to when you feel lacking in creativity.

Fun Fact:

Did you know that the Unicorn is said to have created all the colours of the rainbow? Legend has it that before the Unicorn, the world was black and white!

Unicorn Spell for Being Brave

What you'll need:

* 1 crystal chalice (or drinking glass)
* Access to a ravine (or tap)
* An open space
* A piece of paper
* A pen

What to do:

Done correctly, this spell will harness enough of the bravery of the Unicorn to see you through life. Begin by going outdoors (outdoor space will work best for this spell). Before starting the spell, take a few deep breathes of the fresh air, let your worries and fears leave with each exhale. Take your pen and paper, and write a list of things that you want to achieve but are too fearful to do. With your list complete, simply stand up and let the piece of paper drift off on the wind (pick it up later to avoid littering!). Complete your spell by taking a drink from your crystal chalice of ravine water (tap water from a glass) - this embodies the bravery spell you have just completed and will allow you to achieve your list of goals with a new found sense of bravery and determination.

Fun Fact:

Did you now that the Unicorn is said to be the bravest of all creatures? Many stories state that it is the lion which is the bravest animal, but in fact it is the Unicorn who has no fears, no matter what the situation.

Unicorn Spell for Bringing Luck

What you'll need:

- 1 lucky horseshoe (or a drawing of one should also work!)
- 1 scented candle (smell of your choice)
- 1 bouquet of roses plucked from the Unicorn's field (or a bunch of flowers from your local florist should work too)

What to do:

It is well known that the Unicorn is a symbol of luck and wealth. This spell will allow you to take a piece of Unicorn luck and apply it to your own life. Begin by displaying your lucky horseshoe (or the drawing of one) somewhere that can be seen from anywhere in the room. In front of the horseshoe (at a safe distance) light your scented candle and allow the luck from the horseshoe to mingle with the scent of the candle. Whilst this magical aroma is being created, start to place your roses into a desired arrangement and once satisfied, blow out your candle. It may take an hour or even a day but your spell will only be fully complete once the first petal from your roses has fallen.

Fun Fact:

Did you know that the rose is a Unicorn's favourite flower? It is said that the playing fields of the Unicorn are coated in roses of all colours of the rainbow!

Unicorn Spell for Being Artistic

What you'll need:

* 1 large blank canvas
* A set of multi-coloured paints
* 1 paint brush
* A piece of inspirational background music

What to do:

For this spell you are trying to develop your inner 'artist' which will pave the way for all your future artistic ventures. Undertaking this Unicorn spell should allow you to become more creative in everything you do. Begin by taking your blank canvas and setting out your paints and brush, all the while considering what you feel will symbolise your artistic self. Once you have a clear picture in your mind, begin to paint it onto your canvas, ensuring you use multiple colours to inspire creativity and flair for the future. During this time you should allow the inspirational background music to create a sense of strength and calm, the music will help inspire your creative side. Once your painting is complete and dry, place it up high on a wall or shelf so that it can be seen every day. This constant reminder of creativity and possibility will keep the spell working long-term.

Fun Fact:

Did you know that a Unicorn's favourite pastime is to paint? Unicorns love experimenting with colours and textures to create new and interesting works of art, each one as magic as the last.

20

Unicorn Spell for Being Successful

What you'll need:

½ teaspoon of dried mint leaves
1 tablespoon of boiling water
A small bowl
2 drops of essential oils

What to do:

According to Unicorn law the key to true success in any part of life can be created from within. This spell will enhance your dormant strength and help you to get what you desire. Begin by putting the dried mint leaves into a small bowl, topping this off with 1 tablespoon of freshly boiled water. Allow the fresh aroma to fill the air as you consider you goals and what you aim to succeed in. Add two drops of essential oil to the liquid, breathe deeply and as you do so allow the aroma to release any apprehension you have been keeping hold of. You can keep your spell active to provide on-going motivation as your goal approaches.

Fun Fact:

Did you know that every Unicorns suceeds in every aspect of their life? To date there is no record of a failed Unicorn in the history of Unicorns.

Unicorn Spell for Conquering Fears

What you'll need:

* A mirror
* 3 tea-light candles
* 3 pieces of paper and a pen

What to do:

For this spell you want to conjure up your biggest fears in order to combat them. The spell works for up to three fears at one time. Begin by lighting all three candles (if you have three fears, two if only two and one if just one fear). Once lit, take your paper and lay each piece out, all the while you must have your mirror in front of you so you can see yourself, your paper and candles in the reflection. Begin by writing out one fear onto a piece of paper, repeat this with the other two if you have more than one. This spell will work best if you say the fear out loud whilst concentrating hard on WHY you are frightened of this thing. Repeat the fear once more and blow out the corresponding flame. By extinguishing the light you are disregarding this fear, meaning you can tackle it head on. Repeat this for any others fears you have. End the spell by ripping your pieces of paper in half. Your spell is now complete and you can face your fears.

Fun Fact:

Did you know that a Unicorn has no fears at all? It is believed that Unicorns have never known fear of any kind and this has developed into a powerful magic that can assist others in conquering their own fears.

Unicorn Spell for Finding Lost Objects

What you'll need:

A piece of parchment paper from an ancient diary (or a piece of notepad paper)
A quill and ink (or a ballpoint pen)
1 white candle

What to do:

A great ancient Unicorn once said, "Nothing once lost, can't be found". Harnessing the Unicorn powers for this spell will bring back your lost object in its entirety, but requires the utmost level of focus. Begin your spell by dimming the lights and closing any curtains and blinds - you need only the light from a single candle to illuminate your space. Taking your piece of ancient parchment paper (notepad paper) take 5 minutes to really focus on the blank canvas, with nothing in your mind except the object you have lost. Now, taking your quill and ink (pen), write out the name of that which you seek. Gently fold your paper into four pieces, and place it underneath your candle holder. Once your flame is blown out the object should return to you within 24 hours.

Fun Fact:

Did you know that the Unicorn has the ability to retrieve any lost or stolen items? It is believed that the Unicorn's ancient powers are stronger than any other creature in the world.

Unicorn Spell for Being Approachable

What you'll need:

* 1 plain t-shirt
* A multipack of fabric paints
* 1 magical paintbrush crafted from the wood of an enchanted tree (or a normal brush should be ok)

What to do:

As the Unicorn's favourite thing in the world is colour, this spell uses both colour and appearance to create a powerful spell for approachability. Begin by laying out your plain t-shirt on a flat surface and think of an image or pattern that you feel is representative of you. Taking your magical brush (or normal one) paint your design onto the t-shirt using your fabric paints (the more colourful the better!) Once you are happy with your creation you must leave it to dry somewhere cool and airy - this will allow the magic to develop quicker. Once your t-shirt is dry you may wear it on your next trip outside. This is when the spell will activate to help people know you are approachable, friendly and a great person to know!

Fun Fact:

Did you know that when a Unicorn is meeting another Unicorn for the first time it displays all the colours of the rainbow across its mane and tail? This let's the other Unicorn know it is approachable and friendly!

Unicorn Spell for Being Understanding

What you'll need:

- Bubble bath of your choice
- 1 tablespoon of lavender oil
- 1 piece of poetry that you relate to

What to do:

The Unicorn is amongst the most peaceful and understanding creatures in the world. This spell will help you become more understanding of others. Begin by filling a bathtub with hot water and the bubble bath of your choice (we recommend chamomile for extra relaxation). Once your bath is full add one tablespoon of lavender oil before getting in. Once you have got settled in your bath take a few moments to let the warmth and aroma encompass you. Close your eyes and think about times in your life when you have not been as understanding as perhaps you could have been. Think about how it made the other person feel and how that made you feel. Allow those negative vibes to be vented during this time and when you are ready open your eyes. Take your piece of poetry and speak the words out loud. Once you have finished you should feel much lighter and at peace with yourself and the world. The spell is now complete and you are ready to look at situations with understanding and calm.

Fun Fact:

Legend says that you can approach a Unicorn with any problem in the world and they will have full understanding of your situation, free of judgement.

Unicorn Spell for Being Minimalistic

What you'll need:

* A box of Unicorn sacks (or bin bags)
* Motivating music

What to do:

Similar to the nature of this spell, you don't need much to get it done. Living a minimalistic lifestyle is very important to a Unicorn. Their law believes that possessions can become overpowering and diminish creativity and happiness. To begin the spell you should play your chosen motivational music - this can be of any genre you feel works best for you. Start by placing a Unicorn sack (bin bag) in each room of your home and then room by room make your way through each space and throw anything you wish to give to charity into the sack (bag). The key throughout the spell is to be ruthless with your items. If you have not used them in over 1 month, could it be better used by someone else? Once you have a bag for charity in each room, go round again with an empty sack to throw any rubbish you don't want away. With each bag filled you will feel the spell working its magic. As your environment becomes cleaner and spacious, so does your mind.

Fun Fact:

Did you know that a Unicorn has no long-term possessions? It is said that a Unicorn can live with nothing and be as free and happy as any creature in the world. When a Unicorn has a possession it only keeps hold of it for a short period of time before passing it on.

Unicorn Spell for Being Tidy

What you'll need:

A Unicorn wall planner (or regular wall planner)
1 magic marker pen (or normal marker pen)
3 magical chests (or storage boxes)

What to do:

This spell is one of the Unicorn's best kept secrets as it is very easy to do but extremely powerful! To be as tidy as a Unicorn, you must begin by setting out your Unicorn wall planner somewhere accessible and on show. Taking your magic marker (pen), write out a weekly tidying schedule that is both easy to follow and realistic for your lifestyle. You will also need three magical chests (or storage boxes) - these will be used to contain anything that you see lying around your house which you do not use every day. The power behind this spell will ensure you make the best use of your items and often leads to a healthy decluttering of unused items. Simply by writing your tidying schedule out on your Unicorn wall planner and by following your storage rules you will find this spell works wonders.

Fun Fact:

Did you know that you will never find a thing out of place in the Unicorn world? The Unicorn is the most tidy and organised creature to ever live, and by following these very same rules they live in a clutter-free world.

Unicorn Spell for Waking Early

What you'll need:

* 1 mug of hot cocoa
* 1 incense stick
* A Unicorn alarm clock (or regular alarm clock will do)
* A sleeping mask made from the hairs of the Unicorn (or a regular cotton one should do)

What to do:

It is common knowledge that the Unicorn rises before the sun each day. For this spell you are going to take some of this Unicorn magic and apply it to your own routine. Begin by making yourself a mug of hot cocoa around 1 hour before you go to sleep (to achieve the best results aim to get at least 8 hours sleep). This spell works best when you take your cocoa to bed with you. Light some incense in your room, get into bed and finish your hot drink. You should finish your drink at the same time as your incense burns out (make sure it is safely extinguished), at which point it is time to set your alarm. Finally take your Unicorn (cotton) sleeping mask and relax into your bed. Let the excitement of tomorrow's possibilities lull you into a deep and peaceful sleep. This spell should allow for you to rise bright and early with a spring in your step!

Fun Fact:

Did you know that when a Unicorn sleeps it dreams about the day ahead? The magic of a Unicorn allows it to see its future during sleep so that it can wake with ease!

38

Unicorn Spell for Willpower

What you'll need:

* A whiteboard
* A marker pen
* An inspirational role model

What to do:

A Unicorn possesses extreme willpower and can achieve whatever they put their minds to. In this spell you will harness the willpower of your role model along with the power of the Unicorn to achieve your willpower goal. Begin by focusing on one key area - this can be anything from losing weight to studying hard! When you have your goal in mind, write it on your whiteboard with the pen. Now looking at the goal in front of you, think about your role model - what would they do to achieve this goal? Harness that inspiration and click your fingers 3 times. Wipe away your goal with your hand and say out loud 'I am strong'. This completes the spell and locks in your inspirational mentality so that you can go out and get what you deserve.

Fun Fact:

Did you know that once a Unicorn sets its mind to something it will do whatever it takes to achieve that goal, regardless of the hurdles it comes across!

Unicorn Spell for Getting the Job!

What you'll need:

* 1 sprig of lucky heather plucked from the fields of the Unicorn Lands (or garden centre)
* 1 small piece of ribbon

What to do:

One of the most common misconceptions around landing your dream job is the notion that who gets selected is out of your control! According to Unicorn law there are things you can do to help your chances of getting the job, aside from the obvious job prep! This spell, which has been plucked from the ancient Unicorn scriptures will help you get an edge over the competition. Start your spell by taking your lucky heather from the Unicorn fields (or garden centre) and take a deep breath in, allowing the lucky aromas to enter your system. As you exhale, take your ribbon and gently tie a bow around the stem of your sprig. To get the most out of this spell you want to ensure that it is kept on your person throughout the interview. For best results keep it with you from the moment the spell is cast until the day you get told the job is yours!

Fun Fact:

Did you know that lucky heather is the most commonly found plant throughout the Unicorn fields? It is believed that the presence of the Unicorn promotes the growth of the luckiest and most beautiful plants in the world.

Unicorn Spell for Loving Yourself

What you'll need:

* A movie of your choice
* 1 blanket made from the hairs of a Unicorn (or cotton)
* A scented candle
* Hand picked strawberries from the Unicorn forest (or shop)

What to do:

Loving yourself begins and ends with you, so this spell will allow you to enhance your abilities when it comes to self-love and self-care. Begin by creating an environment that lends itself to peace and tranquillity, making sure that you wont be interrupted for the duration of the spell. Begin by lighting your scented candle and switching off any other artificial lighting. Allow the smells to fill the room as you start your favourite movie and make yourself comfortable. Consider what it means to you to have this time to yourself, and how it makes you feel. Get underneath your Unicorn blanket (cotton blanket) and indulge in some 'you-time' with hand picked (shop bought) strawberries and your film. The spell is complete once the movie has finished and should leave you feeling happy and content in yourself.

Fun Fact:

Did you know that a Unicorn gains a large portion of it's strength directly from the sun? Laying out in the sunshine help Unicorns 'recharge' their magical batteries.

43

Unicorn Spell for Making A Fresh Start

What you'll need:

* A large bowl
* Freshly boiled water
* 1 lemon
* An empty spray bottle

What to do:

According to Unicorn Law this spell works best during the Spring season when the flowers start to bloom, although it can be done at any time. Begin your spell by opening all the windows of your home to release any trapped negativity or bad feelings. Allow the breeze to blow away the cobwebs as you boil your water. Fill a bowl of boiling water and cut one lemon in half. Squeezing each piece into the water to create a strong citrus aroma, consider what you would like to achieve in the upcoming months and how far you have already come in your life. Allow the lemon-infused water to cool before decanting the mixture into an empty spray bottle. Go around your home, spraying small bursts of fresh lemon water to create a fresh and clean scent. With each room you visit allow yourself to leave the past behind to make way for the future. Once you have visited every room, take a few minutes to breathe in the promising aromas before closing your windows.

Fun Fact:

Did you know that Springtime is the Unicorn's favourite season of all? It is said that Unicorn magic is at its most powerful during the Spring months and anything is possible!

Unicorn Spell for Getting Motivated!

What you'll need:

- Page 100 of your favourite book
- A candle
- A pair of maracas
- A pen
- A piece of paper

What to do:

Begin by lighting your candle. Let the warmth from the flame fill the room, take a deep breath in and exhale gently. Start the spell off by reading each word from page 100 of your favourite book out loud. As you read, let your mind absorb the words, find the meaning behind them and let the words inspire you. Once you have finished reading, grab your pen and piece of paper; it is now time for the main part of the spell! Without thinking too deeply, make a list on your paper of all the things you want to achieve, and why you want to achieve them. Use this time to think about your role models, what is it about them that inspires you, and what do you need to do to get closer to this goal? Pick up your maracas and gently shake them once, pause, and a second time. With those words fresh in your mind, and the feelings of motivation buzzing through your body, seize the day, and take the first step to achieving your dreams!

Fun Fact:

Did you know that the Unicorn is a symbol of trust? The next time you come face to face with a Unicorn, know you have been blessed with the gift of unyielding trust in others.

47

Unicorn Spell for Making Friends

What you'll need:

* 10 cupcakes topped with chocolate sprinkles
* 10 hand-crafted boxes (or cardboard boxes)
* 10 Unicorn greeting cards

What to do:

The Unicorn makes friends immediately due to its magical aura. For this spell you will be able to absorb a little of this magic into each cupcake to deliver to 10 potential new friends! Begin by unpacking your 10 cupcakes (these can be bought or homemade!) and place each one inside a handcrafted box (or cardboard box) for delivery. Before sealing each box, hand-write a Unicorn greeting card to include with your delivery. This card should be well thought out, you must consider what you want your new friends to know about you and why they might want to get to know you! Package each cupcake and greeting card inside the boxes ready to go out to your 10 chosen new friends. Inside each box the spell will remain sealed until opened by the recipient at which time it will be released.

Fun Fact:

Did you know Unicorn's make the best friends? It is said to be friends with a Unicorn means never being sad or lonely ever again. The spell of making friends through Unicorn magic ensures lifelong friendship.

Unicorn Spell for Being Positive

What you'll need:

- 6 large handfuls of soil
- 1 flower seed from a Unicorn's field (or your local garden centre)
- ½ cup of Unicorn tears, (or tap water)
- 1 plant pot

What to do:

Positivity grows when you can see progress, and this spell guarantees positivity will grow each and every day right in your own home. Begin by taking your plant pot, and one by one add 3 handfuls of soil. With each handful think one positive wish that you would love to happen. At the halfway point, take your magical seed and place it softly into the soil, topping it off with the remainder of your soil. Before adding your water. Take a moment to consider the enormity of your spell. You are creating life and with that life comes overwhelming strength of positivity. Finish your spell by adding your ½ cup of Unicorn tears (water).

Fun Fact:

Did you know that when a Unicorn cries, the tears are a magical mixture of every colour of the rainbow! It is believed that 1 teardrop from a Unicorn possesses a lifetime of magic.

Unicorn Spell for Challenging Yourself

What you'll need:

* A pair of walking shoes
* A playlist of inspirational music
* A bottle of fresh water
* 2 lemon wedges from the Unicorn Forest lemon tree (or your local shop)

What to do:

To begin this spell take two wedges of lemon and add them to a bottle of fresh cold water. This will signify fresh and natural beginnings for you during the spell. Take your walking shoes and a playlist of inspirational music to play along the way. This specific spell involves nature as the Unicorns live out in the wild and challenge themselves on a daily basis. Take your water and music then venture out the door for your walk. The walk can take you on any route or path, but it must be a new adventure, so a new route that has never been taken before is best. During your walk try thinking clearly about the sorts of goals you have, especially focusing on those that you feel may be too difficult. Throughout this walk you must constantly sip from your lemon-infused water bottle, remembering that you can conquer anything you put your mind to! This spell is complete upon arriving home, by which time you will have finished your magical water.

Fun Fact:

Unicorns love to create challenges both for themselves and their friends to complete as they are very competitive.

Unicorn Spell for Being Productive

What you'll need:

1 chalkboard
A piece of chalk
A piece of fabric from the cloak of an ancient God (or a piece of kitchen roll will do)

What to do:

For this spell you will need to harness the strength from the Unicorns to focus your attention upon your goals. To begin with, consider 5 things you want to achieve today, then taking your piece of chalk write out your list of goals. This part is important as it ensures the ideas become a reality by placing them in view. The Unicorn states that a goal can only become a reality if you make it tangible. Once you have your written goals, take a moment to consider 3 steps needed to achieve each one. As you make your way through the list, use your ancient fabric (kitchen roll) to wipe away the goal. By doing this you have committed your ambitions to your brain, which completes the spell and allows you to achieve.

Fun Fact:

Did you know that the Unicorn is able to achieve up to 100 goals in 1 hour? It is said that the power and speed of a Unicorn is unmatched by any other living being. It is for this reason that the Unicorn is such a powerful symbol for productivity.

Unicorn Spell for Being Intelligent

What you'll need:

* A Unicorn dictionary (or a normal one should do)
* A Unicorn calendar
* 7 pieces of magic chocolate (or regular chocolate will work)

What to do:

The Unicorn is the most intelligent creature in the world - there is nothing a Unicorn does not know. For this spell you will take a slice of Unicorn intelligence to use in your daily life. Start by picking out 7 words that you do not know from your Unicorn Dictionary (this is important, they must be new words to you!) Write out one word into each day of the week on your calendar, it is best to only do one week at a time, however you can do more if you wish. Each day that rolls around will be dedicated to the new word, you must use it at least 3 times throughout your day and at the end of each day you must be able to say exactly what it means. Once this has been achieved, you may eat one piece of magical chocolate to seal the spell. By following this plan each week you are constantly enhancing the spell to make it more and more powerful over time.

Fun Fact:

Did you know that a Unicorn can tell you the meaning of every word in the dictionary? It is said that one of the the Unicorn's favourite past times is to constantly learn and use brand new words!

Unicorn Spell for Getting Active

What you'll need:

1 peeled banana
2 apples from the orchid of the Unicorn forest
(or your local shop)
1 cup of water from the forest springs
(or tap water should do)
A blending device
1 teaspoon of liquid Unicorn energy (or peanut butter)

What to do:

The Unicorn is one of the most active creatures in the world with unlimited levels of energy. This spell should transfer some of this power over to you! Start by gathering your crucial ingredients and begin by putting your banana inside your blender. Whilst you are adding each ingredient, consider the last time you felt really active, and how that made you feel. Add two apples (chopped with pips removed) from the orchid of the Unicorn forest (or shop) and place a teaspoon of liquid Unicorn energy (peanut butter) inside. Finish the mixture off with a cup of water from the forest springs (tap) and blend until smooth. Take a sip and think of one activity you would like to do each day for the next week. Close your eyes. Sip again. Now go out and take life by the horns!

Fun Fact:

Did you know that the Unicorn can run up to 10 marathons a day as it possesses the most stamina of all the world's creatures!

Unicorn Spell for Getting Organised

What you'll need:

* 10 Unicorn themed stickers
* A Unicorn calendar
* A silk ribbon from the Unicorn's treasure chest (or a piece of string)
* 4 coloured pens (choice is yours)

What to do:

Using the stationary of the mystical Unicorn anybody can create a spell for high levels of organisation! To get started you need your calendar turned to the present month and in order to maximise your planning potential, ensure the rest of your equipment is laid out. Taking your first coloured pen, write the appropriate tasks you need to achieve in their correct days. Using a second colour write in any social activities you have planned then with the third you need to input any work deadlines. Finally with your fourth you are to write some inspirational messages that will boost your motivation throughout the month. Now using your magical silk ribbon (or string), tie a loop through the top of your calendar and hang it up somewhere prominent. When each task if complete, place a Unicorn sticker in the square. These methods will enhance the power of your spell to ensure that you are achieving high levels of organisation every day!

Fun Fact:

One of the Unicorn's favourite things is colour, and in order to always be organised, it uses colour coordination to plan it life.